The Cartographer Tries to Map a Way to Zion

Kei Miller was born in Jamaica in 1978. He earned an MA in Creative Writing at Manchester Metropolitan University and a PhD in English Literature at the University of Glasgow, where he is now Reader and teaches Caribbean Literature and Creative Writing. Kei won the Caribbean Rhodes Trust Fellowship in Cultural Studies in 2013 and the Silver Musgrave Medal from the Institute of Jamaica. He has published books of fiction, essays and poetry.

Also by Kei Miller from Carcanet Press

There is an Anger that Moves
A Light Song of Light

As editor

New Caribbean Poetry: An Anthology

KEI MILLER

The Cartographer Tries to Map a Way to Zion

Acknowledgements

Versions of some of these poems have previously appeared in *Caribbean Beat*, *The Dark Horse* and *Draconian Switch*. The poem 'Place Name: Edinburgh Castle' was written as a commission for the Empire Café for the Glasgow Commonwealth Games, 2014.

The writing of this collection was largely made possible thanks to the Caribbean Rhodes Trust and, specifically, the Rex Nettleford Fellowship in Cultural Studies which the trust awarded me.

I livicate these poems to the bredrens and sistrens of 'Occupy Pinnacle', still fighting for Zion, still fighting for a rightful portion of land.

First published in Great Britain in 2014 by
Carcanet Press Limited
Alliance House
Cross Street
Manchester M2 7AQ

www.carcanet.co.uk

A CIP catalogue record for this book is available from the British Library

ISBN 978 1 84777 267 1

The publisher acknowledges financial assistance from Arts Council England

Supported by
**ARTS COUNCIL
ENGLAND**

Typeset by XL Publishing Services, Exmouth

She hope dem caution worl–map
Fi stop draw Jamaica small
For de lickle speck cyaan show
We independantness at all!

Moresomever we must tell map dat
We don't like we position –
Please kindly tek we out a sea
An draw we in de ocean

– Louise Bennett

Any any where Rastafari trod
Any any where Rastafari trod
Any any where Rastafari trod
Babylon a follow

Only one place him cannot trod
Only one place him cannot trod
Only one place him cannot trod
Holy Mount Zion

– Rastafari chant

Contents

Groundation

So begin this thing
with an *Abu ye! Abu ye! Abu ye!*
A heartbless. Step out
from the case of your sandals,
stand shoeless. Allow your knees
and then your forehead an intimacy
with stone; know your ground.
The emperor that landed here
in 1966 was led down his ites
and gold and green plane
by a rastaman. And tell me,
was it all for show –
the way he scorned
the red rolled out for him?
He walked, instead, on common
ground – the hem of Selassie's trousers
brushed the dust of Babylon.
Reach through history; touch
this kneeling crowd – the tarmac
soft against the substance of its faith.

The Shrug of Jah

                              In the long ago beginning
                              the world was unmapped.
It was nothing really –
            just a shrug of Jah
something he hadn't thought   all the way through
Our world was neither here   nor there
                        with him
and neither   here nor there
                  with itself.
      A world
            which did not know
                        if it would stay
                        or go.
            No.

                        or go.
                        if it would stay
            which did not know
      A world
                        with itself.
and neither   here nor there
                  with him
Our world was neither here   nor there
something he hadn't thought   all the way through
                  just a shrug of Jah.
It was nothing really –

                        the world was unmapped.
                        In the long ago beginning

Establishing the Metre

Like tailors who must know their clients' girths
    two men set out to find the sprawling measure of the earth.
    They walked the curve from Rodez to Barcelona,
    and Barcelona to Dunkirk. Such a pilgrimage!
    They did not call it inches, miles or chains —
    this distance which as yet had no clear name.
    Between France and Spain they dared to stretch
    uncalibrated measuring tapes. And foot
    by weary foot, they found a rhythm
    the measure that exists in everything.

Quashie's Verse

But what now
is the length
of Quashie's
verse? He
who can no longer
measure by *kend* or by
chamma or by *ermijja*; he who
knew his poems by how they fit
in earthenware, perfect as water,
words shaping themselves against red
clay grooves. And though no two jars were
precisely like each other – it worked for Quashie
– this 'just about' measure – for words are like that –
each one carrying its own distance. Even this, despite
its best shaping efforts, will never quite be a
jar. So what now shall Quashie do – his old
measures outlawed, and him instructed
now in universal forms, perfected by
universal men who look nothing
and sound nothing
like Quashie?

Unsettled

So consider an unsettled island.
Inside – the unflattened and unsugared

fields; inside – a tegareg
sprawl of roots and canopies,

inside – the tall sentries of blood-
wood and yoke-wood and sweet-wood,

of dog-wood, of bullet trees so hard
they will one day splinter cutlasses,

will one day swing low the carcasses
of slaves; inside – a crawling

brawl of vines, unseemly
flowers that blossom from their spines;

inside – the leh-guh orchids and labrishing
hibiscuses that throw raucous

syllables at crows whose heads are red
as annattos; inside – malarial mosquitoes

that rise from stagnant ponds;
inside – a green humidity thick as mud;

inside – the stinging spurge, the night-
shades, the Madame Fates;

inside – spiders, gnats and bees,
wasps and lice and fleas; inside –

the dengue, the hookworm, the heat
and botheration; unchecked macka

sharp as crucifixion. This is no paradise –
not yet – not this unfriendly, untamed island –

this unsanitised, unstructured island –
this unmannered, unmeasured island;

this island: unwritten, unsettled, unmapped.

What the Mapmaker Ought to Know

On this island things fidget.
Even history.
The landscape does not sit
willingly
as if behind an easel
holding pose
waiting on
someone
to pencil
its lines, compose
its best features
or unruly contours.
Landmarks shift,
become unfixed
by earthquake
by landslide
by utter spite.
Whole places will slip
out from your grip.

The Cartographer Tries to Map a Way to Zion

i. in which the cartographer explains himself

You might say
my job is not
to lose myself exactly
but to imagine
what loss might feel like –
the sudden creeping pace,
the consultation with trees and blue
fences and whatever else
might prove a landmark.
My job is to imagine the widening
of the unfamiliar and also
the widening ache of it;
to anticipate the ironic
question: how did we find
ourselves here? My job is
to untangle the tangled,
to unworry the concerned,
to guide you out from cul-de-sacs
into which you may have wrongly turned.

ii. in which the rastaman disagrees

The rastaman has another reasoning.
He says – now that man's job is never straight-
forward or easy. Him work is to make thin and crushable
all that is big and as real as ourselves; is to make flat
all that is high and rolling; is to make invisible and wutliss
plenty things that poor people cyaa do without – like board
houses, and the corner shop from which Miss Katie sell
her famous peanut porridge. And then again
the mapmaker's work is to make visible
all them things that shoulda never exist in the first place
like the conquest of pirates, like borders,
like the viral spread of governments

iii.

The cartographer says
                no —
What I do is science. I show
the earth as it is, without bias.
I never fall in love. I never get involved
with the muddy affairs of land.
Too much passion unsteadies the hand.
I aim to show the full
of a place in just a glance.

iv.

The rastaman thinks, draw me a map of what you see
then I will draw a map of what you never see
and guess me whose map will be bigger than whose?
Guess me whose map will tell the larger truth?

v.   in which the rastaman offers an invitation

Come share with I an unsalted stew
an exalted stew of gungo peas and callaloo
and let I tell you bout the nearby towns
the ways and chains that I-man trod
how every road might buck yu toe
down here in Babylon.

vi.
after Kai Krause

For the rastaman – it is true – dismisses
too easily the cartographic view;
believes himself slighted
by its imperial gaze. And the ras says
it's all a Babylon conspiracy
de bloodclawt immappancy of dis world –
maps which throughout time have gripped like girdles
to make his people smaller than they were.

vii.

But there are maps
and then again, there are maps;
for what to call the haphazard
dance of bees returning
to their hives but maps
that lead to precise
hibiscuses, their soft
storehouses of pollen?
And what to call the blood
of hummingbirds but maps
that pulse the tiny bodies across
oceans and then back?
And what are turtles born with
if not maps that break
eggs and pull them up from sand
guide them towards ocean instead of land?

viii.

I&I overstand, for is true that I-man
also look to maps drawn by Jah's large hands
him who did pull comets cross the sky
to lead we out from wicked Pharaoh's land.
At noon when sun did hide the high
graph of stars, the cosmic blueprint
of I&I freedom, is Jah who point our eyes
to well-bottom an say *blink and blink until*
you see again the spread of guiding galaxies.
Babylon science now confirm – stars too
are 'black bodies'. I&I did done know this
already – that up there is Jah-Jah's firmament
full of light and livity.

A Prayer for the Unflummoxed Beaver

so unmoved by the boat's slow approach – the boat
drifting across the flat green acre of water; a prayer
for these acres of water which, in the soft light, seem firm;
the squirrels, however, are never taken in;
a prayer for the squirrels and their unknowable
but perfect paths; see how they run across
the twisting highway of cedars but never crash;
a prayer for the cedars and their dead knees rising
from the water like tombstones; a prayer for the cedar balls
that break when you touch them and stain
your fingers yellow, that release from their tiny bellies
the smell of old churches, of something holy;
a prayer returned to the holy alligators – you owe them
that at least, for just last night when you thought
of Hana Andronikova you asked them to pray
with you, knowing that their prayers are potent;
at night the grass is full of their red eyes; a prayer
for the grass which the alligators divide
in the shape of a never-ending S; you lean over
to pull some into the boat; in Burma
this is called ka-na-paw, and can be cooked
with salt and oil; a prayer for the languages
we know this landscape by; for the French
as spoken by fat fishermen, the fat fishermen
who admit to the water – *We all dying.*
You understand? Savez? A prayer
for the dying that will come to all of us
but may it come soft as a boat drifting across the bayou.
May it find us unrattled and as unflummoxed as the beaver.

For Hana Andronikova (1967–2011)

ix.   in which the cartographer travels lengths and breadths

Give him time and he will learn the strange
ways and names of this island: the clapping ascent
to Baptist; the thankful that takes you up Grateful Hill –
Grateful Hill just round the corner from Content; will know
the rough and proud to Boldness and Blackness;
the painful chains to Bad Times; the long and short
to Three Miles, Six Miles, Nine Miles, Eleven Miles
whose distances, incidentally, are unrelated
to each other; he'll know the haunting that takes you
through Duppy Gate; the slow that goes to Wait-a-Bit;
the correct etiquette to Accompong, even to
Me-No-Sen-You-No-Come; will know the grunting path
to Hog Hole; the struggle required for Effort; the potholed
roads to Shambles, Rat Trap and Putogether Corner;
as well, the cartographer will know places named
after places – how this island spreads out as a palimpsest
of maps: for here is Bethlehem; here is Tel Aviv; here
is Gaza; also Edinburgh; Aberdeen; Egypt; Cairo;
and here is Bengal; Mount Horeb; Albion; Alps;
they say – all of here is Babylon.

Place Name

Me-No-Sen-You-No-Come. In plain english: do not enter
without invitation. For consider the once-upon-a-time
adventures of rude pickney answering to name
Goldilocks – nuff-gyal, self-invited into house of bears,
assumed at once her colonial right to porridge, to beds
and to chairs. The baff-hand child went in just so, not
even a token offering of honey, and just like that
proceeded to bruck up things. If only she had pennied
the secret names of places. Me-no-sen-you-no-come:
without invitation, you're not welcome. Or else, come
in as you please – just know that this ground, these
bushes, these trees observe you with suspicion many
centuries deep.

x.   in which the cartographer asks for directions

Sometimes the cartographer gets frustrated when he asks an I-formant how to get to such and such a place, and the I-formant might say something like –

> Awrite, you know the big white house at the bottom of Clover Hill with all the windows dem board up, and with a high shingle roof that look almost like a church?

Yes, the cartographer says.

> And in front the house you always see a ole woman, only three teeth in her mouth, and she out there selling pepper shrimp in a school chair with a umbrella tie to it. And beside her she always have two mongrel dog and one of them is white and the nedda one is brown?

Yes, I know exactly where you mean, the cartographer says.

> And in the yard there is a big guinnep tree that hang right out to the road, so school pickney always stop there to buy shrimp and eat free guinnep?

Yes, yes, the cartographer insists. I know it.

> Good, says the I-formant. Cause you mustn' go there.

xi.

At other times he is amazed
by the hems and haws
        and shrugs of our roads –
        how they never run sure, but seem
                to arc, bend or narrow, just so
                an avenue will turn on itself

as if to give you back a place
you have just come from.
        Lady Musgrave's Road was laid
        in its serpentine way
                so that Miss Musgrave
                on her carriage ride home

would not have to see
a nayga man's property
        so much bigger than her husband's
        own, she did not want to feel
                the carriage slow and know
                her driver had just then turned

his face to Devon House,
a thing wet like pride in his eyes,
        and nodding to himself *yes,*
        is Missa Stiebel build dat. And to think
                that such spite should pass
                down even to the present

generation – should dictate
the thoughtless,
        ungridded shape of our city,
        the slowness of traffic each evening –
                to think that one woman's pride
                should add so much to our daily

commute – this is something
the cartographer does not wish
     to contemplate. Still, he wonders
     if on his map he made our roads a little
         smoother, a little straighter, as if in drawing
         he might erase a small bit of history's disgrace.

A Ghazal for the Tethered Goats

Sometimes in Jamaica, the roads constrict like throats
and around each green corner – the tethered goats.

They are provision from a god that craves
the sacrifice of sons. If not, the tethered goats.

They bleat all night who did not know the size
of abbe seeds and their own beings – these tethered goats.

They do not go to war but send their skins.
How sweet, the repercussion of tethered goats.

Kids tremble at the sound of gumbeh drums
and of their futures. How meek the tethered goats.

Their bellies run for sweetness, and their mouths
are full of awful doom – these tethered goats.

But how they stipple this island, from Trelawny
to Saint Ann to Saint Andrew, the tethered goats.

Roads

The secret roads and slaving roads,
the dirging roads, marooning roads.
> Our people sing:
> *Alligator dah walk on road*
> *Yes, alligator dah walk on road*

The cow roads and cobbled roads,
the estate roads and backbush roads.
> Our people sing:
> *Go dung a Manuel Road*
> *Fi go bruck rock stone*

The marl roads and bauxite roads,
the causeway roads and Chinese roads.
> Our people sing:
> *Right tru right tru de rocky road*
> *Hear Charlie Marley call you*

The press-along, the soon-be-done,
the not-an-easy, the mighty-long –
so many roads we trod upon
and every mile, another song.

xii. in which the rastaman begins to feel uncomfortable

So wide is the horizon as seen
from the flung-open windows
of Rose Hall Great House
that one can observe
the clear
curve of the earth.
For the cartographer
the sea becomes
a glittering parabola,
an arc
of shining measure;

for the rastaman it is
an upturned dutch pot,
the one unwittingly shined
by Anansi's wife, a silver tale
of greed in the midst
of famine,
the tragic
fullup of big-men's belly,
the wash-weh
of small people's magic.

xiii.

You see, the rastaman
has always felt uneasy
in the glistening white splendour
of Great Houses; uneasy
with the way others
seem easy inside them,
their eyes that smoothly scan the green canefields
like sonnets,
as if they'd found
a measure of peace
in the brutal
architecture of history.

xiv.

But the cartographer, it is true,
dismisses too easily the rastaman's view,
has never read his provocative dissertation –
'*Kepture Land*' *as Identity Reclamation
in Postcolonial Jamaica.* Hell!
the cartographer did not even know
the rastaman had a PhD (from Glasgow
no less) in which, amongst other things, he sites
Sylvia Wynter's most cryptic essay: *On How
We Mistook the Map for the Territory,
and Reimprisoned Ourselves in
An Unbearable Wrongness of Being...*

Place Name

Swamp, backbush of Moneague, forgotten place until 2003.
'Swamp' it was called, though nothing in that brambled
landscape bore proof of name – nothing to say moisture,
or damp that could set in furniture, no bones of alligators
had been found. They cleared the ground and gridded it
out for houses. One ram goat was duly killed, blood
sprinkled as just-in-case blessing – as if them never know
what Quashie did done know, that old magic measures
don't always work here. Today a Ferris wheel spins on
the bank of a come-back pond. Boat rides are offered to
visitors. Tour guides twang their Hs across wide water:
Welcome ya'll to Swamp – backbush hof Moneague. Forgotten
place huntil 2003. Now, we har sailing hover Helizabeth
Havenue. Now hacross Martin Boulevard; ladies and
gentlemen, below hus in this deep is yards and yards hof grief,
plenty plots of soak-up dreams.

For the Croaking Lizards

who love art more than most, travelling
from painting to painting as one might

through archipelagos; who can predict
pregnancies by falling on top of heads;

whose translucent skins reveal
a green/blue love inside them;

who give of their extremities
most generously to cats; whose routines

are more precise than clocks; who though
hated and hunted, have remained

profoundly unbothered; nights are loud
with the shrugs of lizards.

Place Name

Wait-A-Bit, gateway to cockpit country. Observe the sturdy
Acacia greggii – 'catclaw', 'devil's claw', 'wait-a-minute'
or 'wait-a-bit' tree. Strong macka that can hold yu and
jook yu and draw blood like murder. Place named not
for patience but for landscapes that scrape; name like
bright yellow caution – *careful man! This here is bruising
land.*

xv.

And it's the way
crows will, sometimes,
halo distant trees –
a black-feathered arc

or the way
the bright sea
in places will grow dark –

such things allow
the cartographer to mark
a small island's latitude
of mysteries.

xvi.   in which every song is singing Zion

On evenings when we put pillows
to our ears, trying to mute the sermons
of a thousand deejays broadcast
on boom-boxes across this island,
it is then that every track leads to Zion:
Bob Marley, Luciano, Junior Gong,
Wingless Angels, Delroy Morgan, Buju Banton,
all-a dem dissa chant down Babylon,
all-a dem dissa chant Armagiddeon.
We dream ourselves alone by abandoned rivers.
Oh Missa Man, will you ever understand
why such songs spring from this strange land?

xvii.

The rastaman now begins a nyabinghi beat
      DUP-DUP-dudududu-DUP-DUP
and the cartographer is finally finding his feet
      DUP-DUP-dudududu-DUP-DUP
aching towards a I-ly I-ly place. The rastaman
calls dis a heartbeat riddim, but dis
      DUP-DUP-dudududu-DUP-DUP
is no riddim the mapmaker's heart is
familiar with. No. Ain't nutt'n iambic bout dis.
      DUP-DUP-dudududu-DUP-DUP
So he start fi wonder bout it
      DUP-DUP-dudududu-DUP-DUP
if dis is what was stolen from Quashie?
Is dis the outlawed measure –
      DUP-DUP-dudududu-DUP-DUP
the riddim of cutlass and cane
      DUP-DUP-dudududu-DUP-DUP
the terrible metre of hurricanes?

Place Name

Shotover – so named because our people, little acquainted
with French, could make no sense of *Château Vert*. And
talk truth, Mr Backra, dat was too stoosh a name for
your house. 'Green and fresh,' you said. No – it did just
mildew and old; a house which, like yourself, has since
returned to the fold of Portland's earth. But oh Mr
Backra, if through the muffle of mud you should hear us
traipsing on your ground, one of us asking – *how it come
about, the name?* you will discover that when victims live
long enough they get their say in history: *Well sah* (an
old man answers)*, in dem dere backra days, bucky-master had
was to catch back the runaway slaves, so him would draw for
him long musket and buss gunshot over dere, and gunshot over
dere, shot dissa fly pashie! pashie! all bout de place. And so
comes we get de name.*

Place Name

Corn Puss Gap for the hiker who, lost and hungry, bedded
down each evening to the sound of wild cats screeching.
Our people say: *when trouble tek yu, pickney shirt fit yu,* or,
when tiger ole him eat cockroach. Only proverbs to explain
how the wary wayfarer, short on resources, found the
wherewithal to catch and skin one brindle puss, and then
salt to cure it. Jack Mandora say: carry on your person,
always, salt enough to fix the names of places.

xviii.

He whose job you might remember was not to lose himself
exactly (his words, not mine) is losing himself tonight.
Amongst the I-drens & I-formants he is smoking a chillum
pipe & learning the ease of flight & what a vantage point to see
this island by!
> how her skin is pimpled with green hullocks
> how the hullocks are feathered with bamboo leaves
> how flames of forest burn amongst cashew trees
>> but how fields are now beige with bagasse;
>> how thin rivers choke on carcasses;
>> how a woman stumbles through the hurting
>> night, blade wedged into her back; how birds
>> and bullets pack the purple band of evening
>> and sing the sky to black.

xix.

But the mapmaker is slowly getting lost
in de iya ites of de rastaman's talk, for consider when
de rastaman I-nunciates something like: Map
was just a land-guage written gainst I&I
who never know fi read it – I&I who born
a Jubilee and grow with I granny and eat crackers
for I tea – I&I who got no talent
for cartography. Map was just Babylon's most vampiric
orthography. Better I&I never learn fi overstand
what was nutt'n more than de downpressor's pig latin,
I&I who I-tinually bun fire fi downpressor,
bun fire fi pig, an bun fire fi latin.

xx. in which the cartographer tells off the rastaman

The cartographer sucks his teeth
and says – every language, even yours,
is a partial map of this world – it is
the man who never learnt the word
'scrupe' – sound of silk or chiffon moving
against a floor – such a man would not know
how to listen for the scrupe of his bride's dress.
And how much life is land to which
we have no access? How much
have we not seen or felt or heard
because there was no word
for it – at least no word we knew?
We speak to navigate ourselves
away from dark corners and we become,
each one of us, cartographers.

Place Name

Half Way Tree – half-way between Greenwich and the
   brown barracks of Stony Hill, 90 foot cotton under
   which soldiers could ease boots from swollen feet, catch
   a lickle West Indian breeze. Cue now a sound like
   feathers as letters retrieved from back pockets, their
   contents already known by heart, are unfolded and read
   again – words as fuel for the second portion of
   journeying. And how that arboreal shade could make a
   script more beautiful! So hail now the dearly departed
   half-way tree; the language tree; hail all that was read
   and written underneath; hail the loop of names carved as
   practice onto its wall-thick trunk; hail Mary O'Leary of
   Ulster and Allie Mac Dhughaill of Glasgow – the 'dear
   loves' told to *come, come and smell the fruity rot of this place*;
   hail the tree first mentioned in 1696 which held its
   ground despite hurricanes, earthquakes, and even the
   British; hail tree which from its great height saw an
   island change. It fell in 1866 of good and natural causes.
   There rises now in its place, sepulchre-shaped, the Half
   Way Tree clock.

Place Name

Edinburgh Castle, at which grave and terrible site was once
found 43 gold watches. Also an assortment of clothing:
petticoats, waistcoats, 2 loose smocks of osnaburg, 3
beaver hats, and 1 splendocious red frock – its panniers
so wide, missus must did think she herself was Queen of
some great island. By then the bodies had rotted.
Facsimiled Castle – Jamaican home of Lewis Hutchison,
alias the Mad Doctor, alias the Mad Master, surgeon and
slave-owner, red-haired immigrant who nights found
crouched on towers, squinting one-eyed at pale bodies
that floated like ghosts through the Pedro District
gloaming. O skilful marksman who shot his way deep
into the annals of West Indian history – bestow new title
unto him who had such audacity to aim death at more
than just niggers: Caribbean's first serial killer.

Hymn to the Birds

No, not to the birds
who know better than us
how to hymn their own songs
rather to words

under which they
flock and find their best
arrangements:
to parliaments

of owls: flings of dunlins:
lamentations of swans:
tremblings of finches: charms
of hummingbirds: hills of ruffs:

rushes of pochards: chatterings
of choughs: to walks
of snipes: commotions of coots:
gulps of swallows: quarrels

of sparrows: to peacocks
that strut in ostentations: larks that fly
in exaltations: thrushes that crowd
the red-leafed ground

as mutations: also to
the pityings of turtledoves:
the unkindnesses of ravens: the descents
of woodpeckers: the murders

of crows: a hymn then
not to birds but to words
which themselves feel
like feather and wing

and light, as if it were
on the delicacy of
        such sweet syllables
that flocks take flight.

xxi.

So every night while the mapmaker expands
on his network of secret roads and slaving roads,
marooning roads and backbush roads,
what he has really concerned himself with is Zion –
a question has wedged itself between his learning
and awakening: how does one map a place
that is not quite a place? How does one draw
towards the heart?

Filop Plays the Role of Papa Ghede (2010)

This is my people's measure of long time –
'Dat a from when Wappy kill Filop!'
long ago crime, recounted now in folk
chronometry. Filop, we might imagine,
was once 'Philip', name since rounded out
like river stone by the flow of our creole,
or maybe just the accent of earth
the way a piece of grung might open
its mouth to say the name of one
whose blood it has absorbed.

Recent sighting of Filop takes place
under a June plum tree in Tivoli. He greets
eighty-one duppies that rise like roses
from their bullet-ridden corpses. Walking
towards them, he raises two fingers
to his lips, puffs in and out the vapours
of his ghostly self. 'Well,' he says, 'is dead
all of oonoo dead. Welcome to de dread
circle of carnage – blade to blade, bullet
to bullet, body to body, this is our country.'

Distance

Distance is always reduced at night
The drive from Kingston to Montego Bay is not so far
Nor the distance between ourselves and the stars
And at night there is almost nothing between
The things we say, and the things we mean.

When Considering the Long, Long Journey of 28,000 Rubber Ducks

To them who knew to break free from dark hold of ships

who trusted their unsqueezed bodies instead to the Atlantic;

to them who scorned the limits of bathtubs,

refused to join a chorus of rub-a-dub;

to them who've always known their own high tunes,

hitched rides on the manacled backs of blues,

who've been sailing now since 1992; to them

that pass in squeakless silence over the *Titanic*,

float in and out of salty vortexes; to them

who grace the shores of hot and frozen continents,

who instruct us yearly on the movement of currents;

to those bright yellow dots that crest the waves

like spots of praise: hail.

xxii.
for Ronald Cummings

Look close, says the rastaman, on how my people walk them roads
like sankey, how we press along and press along and never yet
get weary. Or else we walk out boasy, as if a selecta man
has called us forth. Them roads was mapped out by song –
mountain road hold soprano, city lane hold tenor,
them big potholes manage what we call a *Baptist alto* –
sound made by women with names like Elva, B-flatting their ways
through 'A Little More Oil in My Lamp' while the pianoman
                                                                                    plays
in the key of G. Listen nuh, dem roads don't sound no harmony
all like you would used to – fi wi road don't round up
or decent up them mouth. Fi wi road make noise like Rosie
stand up in front of CVM camera. Fi wi road say laaawwd;
fi wi road say woooiii. Fi wi road say reeeyyy! Big chune a play!

xxiii.

The cartographer asks
if not where
then what is Zion?
And the rastaman warms to this
and says:

Zion is a reckoning day
don't make nobody fool yu
Zion is a turble day

is a 'draw for the heavy
ledger Book of Deeds
and scroll through and find
out where all what yu think
you did get weh wid
is recorded' day

is an accounts settling day

is a 'reach deep
inna yu pocket
and pay de bill
cause more than lights
and water
going to get lock off
today' day

Zion is a receipts and payment day

And Zion is a parcel
of land returned onto Natty
day; more than Africa,
more than I-thiopia
but even the little corner
in Mobay dat dem tief

in 1963
to build gas station pon it
till Natty see de transgression
and whisper in him heart
more fire
and de spark from that curse
light de gas pump
that was right then filling
de tank of de Governor's Benz;
and de gas station which
was on the rightful land of Natty
go BOOM
and bun down to de ground
causing Bustamante to call down
edict on all rastaman –
rastaman who in order to survive
the turble wrath of Babylon
had was to hide themselves
in mattresses. O Zion
is Coral Gardens revisited,
a reassembling of every baton
that was broken
on de head of Natty,
now turned onto them
that first wielded those sticks.

Zion is a reckoning day,
don't make nobody fool yu
Zion is a turble day

Is a 'draw de rough stone forward
and sit pon it' day.
Sit in burning audience
with him whose eyes
are like cannonballs
and explain to him please
why yu cut de locks
off of Natty? Or worse
and wussurer, why
you try so hard

to cut de tongue out of Natty,
out of all Zion's children
telling dem how dem words
was rough and uncomely –
how dem language
was nothing more
than a tegareg sound?
Explain why you try so hard
to dub out Natty's poems.

O Zion
it is a turble day
a tunderball and lightening day
a most dreadful day
to them who never sight
Zion coming fast
on the horizon

The rastaman shakes his locks
and says:

I hasten de fall of Babylon

I hasten Armagiddeon

I hasten that which will be redder

than red

and that which will be dreader

than dread

I hasten de day of de fireman

I hasten de day of de I-ya man

I hasten de day of de Lion

I hasten Zion.

xxiv.   in which the cartographer attends Reggae Sumfest

And it came to pass, when Moses held up his hand,
that Israel prevailed: and when he let down his hand,
Amalek prevailed
                              Exodus 17:11

The cartographer who has stood now
for over an hour during Sizzla Kalonji's
phenomenal performance, a reel

of old hits – *Black Woman and Child,*
Rise to the Occasion, Pump Up Har
Pum Pum, Praise Ye Jah –

has watched not Kalonji but
his flagman dutifully waving the ites
gold and green, and without

ever getting a forward. All when
the drummer, the bassist and the keyboarder
have gotten their names mentioned

played each one a solo to the heaving
crowd – and even while each backup singer
was singing her own piece – there he was

a man unacknowledged, his thin
and trembling hands raised
like those of Moses. If asked

the flagman would say:
Zion not so far, mi boss –
is just an arm's length away.

The Blood Cloths

for Carolyn Cooper

Acknowledge then
the ingenuity of women
who, when cornered, fished out
the cloths of their menstruation –
raised them in their hands, red blots
like conquering Japanese flags;

Acknowledge then
the high decibels of men, dashing
through cane, distancing themselves
from such soft, soaked weapons
they had not known
could be formed against them;

And raise then
a cloth against the dark
corners of cane, and a cloth
against such corners
as they still exist today;

And acknowledge then
the staining blood of women
which gave to them victory
shining bright as rubies.

Place Name

Bloody Bay, after the cetacean slaughter. But only evening
   tints this water the deep vermilion of history. In the
   western sky a tilley burns its final portion of oil. And
   now, the dying song of whales. And now, the hibiscus
   sea rolling its dead leviathans, their harpooned bodies
   like giant voodoo dolls.

For Pat Saunders, West Indian Literature Critic, after her Dream

for you who once bolted awake at night
having dreamed the dream where no one
came to write our stories down – no Man-man
to draw the Os of 'schoooool' into eternity;
no sons from Aenon Town, Jamaica to skip
syllables across large water towards their mothers;
no Bee upon a rainy pulpit to exhort we
how we is that which was tossed in fire
and ain't come out yet; for you who dreamed
of cancer in the shape of radios
playing undiagnosed songs in the bellies
of mad women; for you who dreamed a dream
so bad yet could not find a mouth to make
the sound *laaaaaaaaaaaawwwwwwwd:*
please cut each word out of this poem
and lay them as a circle round your sleep
knowing nightmare-giving jumbies, by design,
are forced to read what we leave out for them.
Yes, jumbies too are waiting on language
to come back to them.

xxv.

The cartographer informs the rastaman he is now plotting
a way to Zion and the rastaman shakes his head and says:
always this is the way with you people. My bredda,
you cannot *plot* your way to Zion; you can neither *samfy*
your way or *ginnal* your way or palm Jack Mandora
a pound or a dollar and bribe your way in. You cyaa climb
into Zion on Anancy's web – or get there by boat or plane or car.
Neither low nor high science will get you through
Jah's impressive door; hypsometry naah guh help yu,
geodesy naah guh help yu, the bathymetric figures
of ocean bottom will not help. My bredda,
you have to walk good and trod holy. You have to pass
through a place called Crosses, and a town called Turbulation,
and only when Jah decide you trod the distance he set out
for you to trod, with Ises in your mouth and cleanness
in your heart, only then, my bredda. Only then.

In Praise of Maps

hymn then a song in praise of maps, without which
we could not dream the shapes of countries:
the boot of Italy, the number 7 of Somalia;
without which we could not trace the course of rivers –
feel a papery Mississippi beneath our fingers;
without which pirates would string nylon
down the necks of useless shovels, play them
each night as banjos; without which submarines
would beach themselves like omens –
rusting mermaids on arbitrary beaches;
without which we would walk nomadic distances,
give up the language of men and learn the gekkering
of foxes; we would negotiate with them
each evening a soft space in their dens.

My Mother's Atlas of Dolls

Unable to travel, my mother makes us
promise to always bring back dolls

as if glass eyes could bear sufficient
witness to where she has not been,

the what of the world she has not seen.
She gathers them – cloth and porcelain

pageant – on her whatnot, makes them
stand regal on white doilies, waving

like queens from their high balconies.
Miss Colombia, Miss Holland, Miss Peru

are just a few who observe, unblinking,
the new world about them. I think

of how we arrange the dead like dolls,
set their arms in precise positions,

how we touch their unseeing eyes;
and how they lie so sweetly still

within their perfect boxes.
It may have been the dolls that taught

my mother how to die, how to travel
once again, how to wave goodbye.

Place Name

Flog Man, for them days when man could get nine-and-thirty
just cause he hold his head so high that Missus call him
uppity. Nigger man admit he sometimes feel the curl of
whips, their stinging S's – tips soaked in horse piss –
more than he feel sun on his skin. Flogging was so
common it was odd that they call this place Flog Man,
why not rename the whole damn country Flog Island?
But it had one beating so brutal, no one could cork their
ears from it; both black and white man fail in the long
practice of deafness; years pass like salve but they was still
hearing it, the cow whip flicking up flecks of skin, and
this Mandingo man who they did think was too big, too
proud to ever let eye water grace him eye was bawling
out a bruck-spirit sound even larger than the barrel of
him chest. Blood did sprinkle the ground like anointing
and now people walk by and cringe as memory curl like
S and lash them owna skin.

Place Name

Try See. Full Free come like rain on hot zinc and even
Quashie who years ago loss his perfect balance with his
toes walk straight and proud off that estate. Massa get
compensate for loss of labour (a payout so great it nearly
bankrupt England) but nothing more than himself would
Quashie gain – not to say that isn't plenty, but really?
Nothing for the loss of toes, loss of language, loss of
continent, loss of 400 years? Such tings could have
turned Quashie bitter as susumba if he never decide his
mind to shut his eye and give thanks for what could give
thanks for – this plot of god-back land, this cyaa-grow-a-
goddamn-thing land, this labour-in-vain land, this 'what
to do but try and try fi tun mi hand make fashion' land,
try and try fi tun de tough grung over, try and try see
what might come tomorrow.

What River Mumma Knows

River Mumma knows things –
the underground trod of Hector's Spring,
of One Eye River. The tributaries feed
the red mangroves of Black River.
Over 100 square miles of Great Morass
are stomping ground of River Mumma.
She knows rocks under which
live large colonies of 'shrimp', or 'swims',
depending on how you learnt to say things.
She knows even more than Goby Fish
where in river bottom alligator lives.
Wag Water is her own most sacred home,
secret place where is kept the famous
golden comb. In Drivers River, Manchioneel,
swim three lady manatees who are
to mermaids as chimpanzees are
to man. Some days River Mumma
just sits cool on a bank, waiting
for signs that prove the prehistoric cows
still evolve towards the magic of herself.
Somewhere in Martha Brae lies the body
of Nora – selfish child who refused Dry River
token portion of ackee – small toll
for privilege of crossing; the girl insisted
she would rather dead.
Dry River call her bluff and come dung
heavy pon her head.
But River Mumma knows
not all things ought to be known.
Not all places ought to be found.
She cries 'Abu ye! Abu ye! Abu ye!'
and swims towards her ground.

xxvi. in which the rastaman gives a sermon

The rastaman says: to get to Zion you must begin
　　　　with a heartbless, a small tilt of the head, a nod,
thumbs and index fingers meeting to take the shape of I
　　　　blood, then raised like a badge to I chest, then you say it:
Heartbless. A simple word that don't cost nothing
　　　　to give but is plenty to receive – like sometimes
you meet an I-dren at your door who come not only
　　　　with a gift from his own acreage but also a word:
how well you look, how prosperous, how beautiful
　　　　the likkle children, or the house, how well appointed –
an I-dren with whom hours pass too quickly and who
　　　　upon leaving offers yet another word: how good it was
to see you and for bredrens and sistrens to sit in the simple
　　　　of each other's love, so that it strike you how both
his coming and his going were announced by blessings.
　　　　My bredda, a man like that is already well on his way
to Zion. So begin like that – a heartbless, the old
　　　　rastaman's chanting up of goodness and rightness
and, of course, upfullness – how excellent is that word –
　　　　upfullness – as if it was a thing that could be stored
in the tank of somebody's heart, so that on mornings
　　　　when salt was weighing you down, when
you feel you can't even rise to face Babylon's numbing work,
　　　　you would know, at least, that should the day wring
your heart out like the chamois towels of streetboys,
　　　　then out of it would spring this stored portion
of upfullness, and so anointed by your own storage,
　　　　you would able to face the road which is forever
inclining hardward. Know then that every heartbless
　　　　given is collected by Jah like mickle and muckle,
or like a basketful of cocoa, and comes back to you
　　　　like a dividend. You find your feet at last
straying off the marl roads, the bauxite roads, the slaving
　　　　roads and the marooning roads, and you would be

turning now onto the singing roads and the sweeting
        roads that lift you up to such a place
as cannot be held on maps or charts, a place that does not
        keep still at the end of paths. Know this,
that lions who trod don't worry bout reaching Zion. In time
        is Zion that reach to the lions.

xxvii.   in which the rastaman says a benediction

In leaving
> the rastaman bids you

Mannaz and Respeck
> Izes and protecshun

Upfullness
> He bids you

Guidance and healt
> Inity and Strenth

Bids you, Trod Holy
> To I-ly I-ly I-ly

Mount Zion-I
> Trod Holy.

Notes

'Groundation'
In Rastafari religion, Grounation or Groundation celebrates the 1966 visit of His Imperial Majesty Haile Selassie to Jamaica. On the day of his arrival, throngs of Rastafarians poured onto the airport tarmac, where they chanted 'Abu ye! Abu ye! Abu ye!'

'Establishing the Metre'
As told in Ken Alder's book *The Measure of All Things*, in order to establish the metric system, French cartographers Pierre Méchain and Jean-Baptiste Delambre set out on a seven-year expedition to measure the earth.

'The Cartographer...', vi.
In 'The True Size of Africa: A Small Contribution in the Fight against Rampant Immappancy' Kai Krause defines 'immappancy' (meant to echo 'illiteracy' or 'innumeracy') as the condition of having 'insufficient geographic knowledge'. Krause's design is in conversation with Mercator's projection, which was first published in 1569 and is still popular today. Mercator's projection distorts the size of the African continent; Greenland is shown as similar in size to Africa. In fact, Africa is fourteen times larger.

'The Cartographer...', xii.
In the Jamaican folktalke 'Anancy and the Magic Pot', the trickster spider finds a dirty magic pot that on his instruction becomes full of food. The only rule is that the pot must never be washed. In the midst of a famine, Anancy greedily eats his bellyful from this pot every day, and allows his family to starve, until his wife follows him and finds the pot, but unfortunately washes it, robbing it of its magic.

'The Cartographer...', xix.
This poem quotes almost verbatim from Lorna Goodison's 'Heartease I': 'We with the straight eyes / and no talent for cartography / always asking / "How far is it to Heartease?"'; 'It say / you can read map / even if you born / a Jubilee / and grow with your granny / and eat crackers for your tea' (from *Guinea*

Woman: New & Selected Poems, Carcanet, 2000, pp. 32–33).

'Filop Plays the Role of Papa Ghede (2010)'
This poem makes reference to the 2010 Tivoli incursion, in which soldiers killed 81 residents of the inner-city community of Tivoli Gardens, Kingston, Jamaica. In Haitian culture Papa Ghede is often depicted with a cigar. He is the god of the crossroads who accompanies the newly dead.

'When Considering the Long, Long Journey of 28,000 Rubber Ducks'
On 20 January 1992 a shipping container holding 28,000 bath toys was lost overboard in the Atlantic on its journey from China to the USA. These rubber ducks have since been sighted on shores all around the world and have been tracked by scientists to understand global currents.

'The Blood Cloths'
'Bloodclawt' is a common and potent Jamaican expletive.